50 From the North Beijing Recipes

By: Kelly Johnson

Table of Contents

- Beijing Zhajiangmian
- Lamb Skewers (Yangrou Chuan)
- Old Beijing Noodle Soup
- Pork and Cabbage Dumplings
- Scallion Oil Pancakes
- Beijing Hotpot
- Fried Sauce Rice Cakes
- Steamed Lamb Buns
- Crispy Sweet Potato Sticks
- Cold Sesame Noodles
- Donkey Burger (Lvrou Huoshao)
- Braised Pork Belly Beijing Style
- Savory Soy Milk Soup
- Mustard Greens with Tofu Skin
- Egg and Leek Stuffed Flatbread
- Stir-fried Pork Liver
- Fermented Mung Bean Noodles

- Old Beijing Minced Lamb Soup
- Jujube Sticky Rice Cake
- Beijing-Style Sweet Bean Rolls
- Bingtanghulu (Candied Hawthorn)
- Wok-Seared Lamb with Cumin
- Dry Fried Green Beans
- Pan-Fried Beef Buns
- Soybean Paste Chicken Wings
- Stir-fried Lotus Root
- Crispy Pancake Rolls
- Black Vinegar Wood Ear Salad
- Thick Beijing Corn Porridge
- Duck Egg Fried Rice
- Sweet Sour Spare Ribs
- Braised Eggplant with Garlic
- Beijing-Style Stuffed Tofu
- Steamed Corn Buns (Wotou)
- Five-Spice Boiled Peanuts
- Glass Noodles with Shredded Chicken

- Stir-Fried Beijing Bitter Melon

- Deep Fried Tofu Balls

- Savory Millet Porridge

- Jiaoquan (Fried Dough Rings)

- Grilled Lamb Chops Beijing Style

- Soybean Sprout Stir Fry

- Beijing Mustard Leaf Stir Fry

- Water Chestnut Cakes

- Cold Garlic Eggplant

- Steamed Pork with Rice Powder

- Jujube Red Bean Pudding

- Sweet Glutinous Rice Balls

- Pickled Radish Salad

- Sesame Flatbread Sandwich

Beijing Zhajiangmian (Fried Sauce Noodles)

Ingredients:

- 8 oz thick wheat noodles
- 1/2 lb ground pork
- 3 tbsp fermented soybean paste (yellow or sweet bean)
- 1 tbsp hoisin sauce
- 1 tbsp soy sauce
- 1 tsp sugar
- Cucumber, radish, and scallions (julienned)

Instructions:

1. Cook noodles and set aside.
2. Stir-fry pork until browned. Add all sauces and sugar. Simmer until thick.
3. Serve sauce over noodles with crisp veggies on top.

Lamb Skewers (Yangrou Chuan)

Ingredients:

- 1 lb lamb shoulder, cubed
- 1 tsp cumin
- 1 tsp chili flakes
- 1 tsp salt
- 1 tbsp oil
- Skewers

Instructions:

1. Marinate lamb in oil and spices.
2. Thread onto skewers. Grill or broil until charred and juicy.
3. Serve with extra cumin and chili sprinkle.

Old Beijing Noodle Soup

Ingredients:

- Wheat noodles
- 1/2 cup pork belly, thinly sliced
- Napa cabbage, mushrooms, and tofu
- 4 cups chicken or pork broth
- Soy sauce, vinegar, and garlic

Instructions:

1. Simmer broth with pork belly and veggies.
2. Cook noodles separately.
3. Assemble soup with noodles, broth, and toppings.

Pork and Cabbage Dumplings

Ingredients:

- Dumpling wrappers
- 1/2 lb ground pork
- 1 cup napa cabbage, finely chopped and salted
- 1 tsp ginger, garlic, soy sauce, sesame oil

Instructions:

1. Mix filling and spoon into wrappers.
2. Fold and seal.
3. Steam or pan-fry until golden and cooked through.

Scallion Oil Pancakes

Ingredients:

- 2 cups flour
- 3/4 cup hot water
- Salt, sesame oil
- 1/2 cup finely chopped scallions

Instructions:

1. Mix dough and rest. Roll out, brush with oil, sprinkle salt and scallions.
2. Roll, coil, and flatten. Pan-fry both sides until golden.
3. Serve sliced with soy-vinegar dip.

Beijing Hotpot

Ingredients:

- Thinly sliced lamb or beef
- Assorted mushrooms, tofu, napa cabbage
- Clear or spicy hotpot broth
- Sesame dipping sauce

Instructions:

1. Boil broth in a large pot.
2. Add ingredients table-side, cooking meat and veggies quickly.
3. Dip into sesame sauce and enjoy.

Fried Sauce Rice Cakes

Ingredients:

- Sliced Korean or Chinese rice cakes
- 1/4 lb ground pork
- 2 tbsp sweet bean sauce
- 1 tbsp hoisin
- Garlic, soy sauce

Instructions:

1. Soften rice cakes in hot water.
2. Stir-fry pork, add sauces.
3. Toss rice cakes in sauce until glossy and warm.

Steamed Lamb Buns

Ingredients:

- Dumpling or bao dough
- Ground lamb
- Onion, cumin, ginger, soy sauce

Instructions:

1. Mix lamb filling. Fill small rounds of dough and seal.
2. Steam for 10–12 minutes until fluffy.
3. Serve hot with chili oil.

Crispy Sweet Potato Sticks

Ingredients:

- Sweet potatoes, julienned
- 1 tbsp cornstarch
- Oil for frying
- Salt, five-spice powder

Instructions:

1. Toss sticks with cornstarch.
2. Deep fry until golden and crispy.
3. Season with salt or five-spice.

Cold Sesame Noodles

Ingredients:

- Cold cooked wheat noodles
- 2 tbsp sesame paste or peanut butter
- 1 tbsp soy sauce
- 1 tsp vinegar
- 1 tsp chili oil
- Cucumber shreds and crushed peanuts

Instructions:

1. Whisk sauce ingredients together.
2. Toss noodles in sauce and top with cucumber and peanuts.
3. Chill and serve cold.

Donkey Burger (Lvrou Huoshao)

Ingredients:

- 1 lb donkey meat (or ground beef as substitute)
- 1 tbsp soy sauce
- 1 tbsp hoisin sauce
- 1 tsp five-spice powder
- Chinese flatbread buns (or pita)
- Scallions and cilantro

Instructions:

1. Mince the donkey meat and cook with soy sauce, hoisin, and five-spice powder.
2. Toast flatbread and stuff with cooked meat.
3. Garnish with scallions and cilantro, then serve.

Braised Pork Belly Beijing Style

Ingredients:

- 1 lb pork belly, cut into chunks
- 2 tbsp soy sauce
- 1 tbsp sugar
- 1/4 cup Shaoxing wine
- 2 star anise
- 1 cinnamon stick
- Ginger, garlic

Instructions:

1. Brown pork belly in a pot with ginger and garlic.
2. Add soy sauce, sugar, wine, and spices.
3. Simmer for 1–2 hours until pork is tender and caramelized.

Savory Soy Milk Soup

Ingredients:

- 4 cups unsweetened soy milk
- 1/2 cup tofu, cubed
- 1 tbsp soy sauce
- 1 tbsp sesame oil
- 2 cloves garlic, minced
- 1 tsp chili oil
- Green onions, cilantro, or bok choy

Instructions:

1. Heat soy milk in a pot and add soy sauce, sesame oil, garlic, and chili oil.
2. Add tofu and simmer for 5–10 minutes.
3. Serve hot with greens or herbs.

Mustard Greens with Tofu Skin

Ingredients:

- 1 bunch mustard greens, chopped
- 1/2 cup tofu skin (yuba), shredded
- 1 tbsp soy sauce
- 1 tbsp rice vinegar
- 1 tsp sugar
- 1 tsp sesame oil
- Garlic and ginger

Instructions:

1. Sauté garlic and ginger, then add mustard greens.
2. Stir-fry for a few minutes, then add tofu skin and seasonings.
3. Cook until tender and serve warm.

Egg and Leek Stuffed Flatbread

Ingredients:

- 1 1/2 cups flour
- 1/2 cup water
- 1/2 tsp salt
- 2 eggs, scrambled
- 1 leek, thinly sliced
- 1 tbsp sesame oil

Instructions:

1. Make dough with flour, water, and salt. Roll out into flatbreads.
2. Cook eggs and leek together, then season.
3. Stuff flatbread with egg-leek mixture, fold, and pan-fry until golden.

Stir-fried Pork Liver

Ingredients:

- 1/2 lb pork liver, sliced
- 1 tbsp soy sauce
- 1 tbsp Shaoxing wine
- 1 tsp ginger, minced
- 1 red bell pepper, sliced
- 2 tbsp oil

Instructions:

1. Marinate pork liver in soy sauce and wine for 10 minutes.
2. Stir-fry ginger, bell pepper, and liver until cooked through.
3. Serve hot with rice or noodles.

Fermented Mung Bean Noodles

Ingredients:

- 1/2 lb mung bean noodles (cellophane noodles)
- 2 tbsp soy sauce
- 1 tbsp rice vinegar
- 1 tbsp chili paste
- Garlic, ginger, scallions

Instructions:

1. Boil mung bean noodles until tender, then drain.
2. Sauté garlic and ginger, then add noodles and seasonings.
3. Stir-fry for a few minutes and top with scallions.

Old Beijing Minced Lamb Soup

Ingredients:

- 1/2 lb ground lamb
- 1 tbsp soy sauce
- 1 tbsp hoisin sauce
- 1 onion, diced
- 4 cups beef broth
- 1 tsp cumin

Instructions:

1. Brown lamb with onion and cumin.
2. Add soy, hoisin, and beef broth, then simmer for 20–30 minutes.
3. Serve hot with cilantro or scallions.

Jujube Sticky Rice Cake

Ingredients:

- 2 cups sticky rice (glutinous rice)
- 1/2 cup jujube dates, chopped
- 1/4 cup brown sugar
- 2 tbsp sesame seeds

Instructions:

1. Steam sticky rice until soft.
2. Mix with chopped jujubes, brown sugar, and steam again.
3. Press into a mold and sprinkle with sesame seeds before serving.

Beijing-Style Sweet Bean Rolls

Ingredients:

- 2 cups red bean paste
- 1 package Chinese pancake rolls (or crepes)
- 1 tbsp sesame oil

Instructions:

1. Spread a thin layer of red bean paste onto the pancake rolls.
2. Roll tightly and steam until warmed through.
3. Brush with sesame oil before serving.

Bingtanghulu (Candied Hawthorn)

Ingredients:

- 12 hawthorn berries (or strawberries if unavailable)
- 1 cup sugar
- 1/4 cup water

Instructions:

1. Thread hawthorn berries onto skewers.
2. In a pan, dissolve sugar in water and boil until syrupy.
3. Dip berries into syrup and let cool until the candy hardens.

Wok-Seared Lamb with Cumin

Ingredients:

- 1 lb lamb, sliced thinly
- 2 tbsp cumin seeds
- 2 tbsp soy sauce
- 1 tbsp chili flakes
- 2 tbsp oil
- 2 cloves garlic, minced
- 1 onion, sliced

Instructions:

1. Heat oil in a wok and sear lamb until browned.
2. Add garlic, onion, cumin seeds, and chili flakes, stir-fry for 2–3 minutes.
3. Season with soy sauce, and cook for another 3–4 minutes until fragrant.
4. Serve hot with rice or flatbread.

Dry Fried Green Beans

Ingredients:

- 1 lb green beans, trimmed
- 2 tbsp soy sauce
- 2 cloves garlic, minced
- 1 tbsp chili paste
- 1 tbsp oil

Instructions:

1. Heat oil in a wok and sauté garlic.
2. Add green beans and dry-fry, stirring occasionally, until they blister and soften.
3. Add soy sauce and chili paste, tossing until coated and fragrant.
4. Serve as a side dish or appetizer.

Pan-Fried Beef Buns

Ingredients:

- 1 lb ground beef
- 1/2 onion, finely chopped
- 1 tbsp soy sauce
- 1 tsp ginger, grated
- 1 tbsp sesame oil
- 1 package of bao or dumpling dough

Instructions:

1. Cook beef with onion, soy sauce, ginger, and sesame oil until browned.
2. Roll dough into small rounds and fill with beef mixture.
3. Seal, then pan-fry in a lightly oiled skillet until golden and crispy on both sides.
4. Serve hot with soy dipping sauce.

Soybean Paste Chicken Wings

Ingredients:

- 10 chicken wings
- 2 tbsp soybean paste (fermented)
- 1 tbsp soy sauce
- 1 tbsp honey
- 1 tsp sesame oil
- 1 tbsp rice vinegar

Instructions:

1. Marinate chicken wings with soybean paste, soy sauce, honey, sesame oil, and vinegar for at least 30 minutes.
2. Bake or grill the wings until crispy and golden.
3. Serve with a side of pickled vegetables or steamed rice.

Stir-Fried Lotus Root

Ingredients:

- 1 lotus root, peeled and sliced
- 1 tbsp soy sauce
- 1 tbsp rice vinegar
- 1 tsp sugar
- 2 tbsp oil
- 2 cloves garlic, minced

Instructions:

1. Heat oil in a pan, sauté garlic, and add lotus root slices.
2. Stir-fry until lotus root becomes tender but still crunchy.
3. Add soy sauce, rice vinegar, and sugar, and toss to coat.
4. Cook for another 2–3 minutes, then serve hot.

Crispy Pancake Rolls

Ingredients:

- 2 cups all-purpose flour
- 1/2 cup water
- 1/4 cup sesame oil
- 1/2 cup finely chopped scallions
- Salt to taste

Instructions:

1. Mix flour, water, and salt to form a dough. Let it rest for 30 minutes.
2. Roll the dough into a thin pancake, then brush with sesame oil and sprinkle with scallions.
3. Roll up the pancake and then flatten it into a circle.
4. Pan-fry until golden and crispy, then slice and serve.

Black Vinegar Wood Ear Salad

Ingredients:

- 1 cup wood ear mushrooms, soaked
- 2 tbsp black vinegar
- 1 tbsp soy sauce
- 1 tsp sugar
- 1/2 tsp sesame oil
- 1 clove garlic, minced
- 1 tbsp chopped cilantro

Instructions:

1. Boil wood ear mushrooms in water for 5 minutes, then drain.
2. Mix black vinegar, soy sauce, sugar, sesame oil, and garlic to make the dressing.
3. Toss mushrooms in the dressing and garnish with cilantro.
4. Serve chilled or at room temperature.

Thick Beijing Corn Porridge

Ingredients:

- 1 cup cornmeal
- 4 cups water or broth
- 1 tbsp sugar
- 1/4 cup corn kernels
- 1/4 cup milk (optional)

Instructions:

1. Bring water or broth to a boil, then slowly add cornmeal, whisking constantly.
2. Cook until it thickens to a porridge consistency, about 10–15 minutes.
3. Stir in sugar and corn kernels, and add milk for a creamier texture.
4. Serve warm as a hearty breakfast or side dish.

Duck Egg Fried Rice

Ingredients:

- 2 cups cold cooked rice
- 2 duck eggs (or regular eggs)
- 1/2 cup peas and carrots
- 2 tbsp soy sauce
- 2 tbsp oil
- 1 clove garlic, minced
- 2 green onions, sliced

Instructions:

1. Heat oil in a wok and scramble the duck eggs.
2. Add garlic, peas, carrots, and rice, stir-fry for a few minutes.
3. Add soy sauce and stir to coat evenly.
4. Garnish with green onions and serve hot.

Sweet Sour Spare Ribs

Ingredients:

- 1 lb spare ribs, cut into sections
- 1 tbsp soy sauce
- 1 tbsp vinegar
- 2 tbsp sugar
- 1/2 cup water
- 1 tbsp cornstarch (optional for thickening)

Instructions:

1. Brown spare ribs in a pot, then remove excess oil.
2. Add soy sauce, vinegar, sugar, and water to the pot, and simmer for 30 minutes.
3. If desired, thicken the sauce with cornstarch.
4. Serve the ribs with the sauce poured over and a side of steamed rice.

Braised Eggplant with Garlic

Ingredients:

- 2 medium eggplants, sliced
- 3 tbsp soy sauce
- 2 tbsp oyster sauce
- 1 tbsp sugar
- 3 cloves garlic, minced
- 1 tbsp sesame oil
- 1/4 cup water
- Green onions for garnish

Instructions:

1. Heat sesame oil in a pan, sauté garlic until fragrant.
2. Add eggplant slices and stir-fry for 5 minutes until they soften.
3. Add soy sauce, oyster sauce, sugar, and water, then cover and braise for 10 minutes.
4. Garnish with chopped green onions and serve hot.

Beijing-Style Stuffed Tofu

Ingredients:

- 1 block firm tofu, drained and sliced
- 1/2 lb ground pork (or beef)
- 1/4 cup bamboo shoots, finely chopped
- 1 tbsp soy sauce
- 1 tbsp hoisin sauce
- 1 tsp five-spice powder
- 1 tbsp cornstarch

Instructions:

1. Hollow out tofu slices, leaving a shell.
2. Mix ground meat, bamboo shoots, soy sauce, hoisin, and five-spice powder, then stuff the tofu.
3. Steam the stuffed tofu for 10–15 minutes.
4. Garnish with chopped scallions and serve.

Steamed Corn Buns (Wotou)

Ingredients:

- 1 1/2 cups cornmeal
- 1 cup flour
- 1 tbsp sugar
- 1 tsp yeast
- 1/2 cup warm water
- 1 tbsp oil

Instructions:

1. Mix cornmeal, flour, sugar, and yeast. Add warm water and knead until smooth.
2. Let the dough rise for 1 hour.
3. Divide into small portions and shape into buns.
4. Steam the buns for 15–20 minutes until fluffy and cooked through.

Five-Spice Boiled Peanuts

Ingredients:

- 2 cups raw peanuts (in shell)
- 2 tbsp soy sauce
- 1 tsp five-spice powder
- 2 dried red chilies
- 1 tbsp sugar
- 4 cups water

Instructions:

1. Boil peanuts in water for 2 hours until soft.
2. Drain and return to the pot.
3. Add soy sauce, five-spice powder, sugar, and dried chilies, then simmer for 20 minutes.
4. Serve warm as a snack.

Glass Noodles with Shredded Chicken

Ingredients:

- 1/2 lb chicken breast, cooked and shredded
- 1 cup glass noodles
- 2 tbsp soy sauce
- 1 tbsp rice vinegar
- 1 tbsp sesame oil
- 1 tsp chili oil
- 1 cucumber, julienned
- 2 green onions, sliced

Instructions:

1. Cook glass noodles according to package instructions.
2. Toss noodles with soy sauce, rice vinegar, sesame oil, and chili oil.
3. Add shredded chicken, cucumber, and green onions, and toss well.
4. Serve chilled or at room temperature.

Stir-Fried Beijing Bitter Melon

Ingredients:

- 1 bitter melon, sliced
- 2 tbsp soy sauce
- 1 tbsp sesame oil
- 1 tbsp rice vinegar
- 2 cloves garlic, minced
- 1 tbsp sugar

Instructions:

1. Heat sesame oil in a wok, sauté garlic until fragrant.
2. Add bitter melon slices and stir-fry for 5 minutes until tender.
3. Add soy sauce, rice vinegar, and sugar, stir well, and cook for another 2 minutes.
4. Serve hot with steamed rice.

Deep Fried Tofu Balls

Ingredients:

- 1 block firm tofu, mashed
- 1/4 cup cornstarch
- 1 egg, beaten
- 2 tbsp soy sauce
- 1 tbsp sesame oil
- 2 tbsp chopped green onions
- Oil for frying

Instructions:

1. Mix mashed tofu, cornstarch, egg, soy sauce, sesame oil, and green onions to form a dough.
2. Shape the dough into small balls.
3. Heat oil in a pan and fry the tofu balls until golden and crispy.
4. Serve with a dipping sauce of soy sauce and vinegar.

Savory Millet Porridge

Ingredients:

- 1 cup millet
- 4 cups chicken or vegetable broth
- 1 tbsp soy sauce
- 1 tbsp sesame oil
- 1/2 cup chopped mushrooms
- 1/4 cup chopped scallions

Instructions:

1. Rinse millet, then cook it in broth until soft, about 20 minutes.
2. Add soy sauce, sesame oil, and mushrooms, then simmer for an additional 5 minutes.
3. Garnish with chopped scallions and serve hot.

Jiaoquan (Fried Dough Rings)

Ingredients:

- 2 cups flour
- 1 tbsp sugar
- 1 tsp baking powder
- 1/2 cup water
- Oil for frying

Instructions:

1. Mix flour, sugar, and baking powder. Add water gradually to form a dough.
2. Roll the dough into long, thin ropes, then join the ends to form rings.
3. Fry the dough rings in hot oil until golden and crispy.
4. Drain excess oil and serve hot, optionally dusted with sugar.

Grilled Lamb Chops Beijing Style

Ingredients:

- 4 lamb chops
- 2 tbsp soy sauce
- 1 tbsp hoisin sauce
- 1 tsp five-spice powder
- 1 tbsp sesame oil
- 2 cloves garlic, minced
- 1 tbsp rice vinegar

Instructions:

1. Marinate lamb chops with soy sauce, hoisin, five-spice powder, sesame oil, garlic, and rice vinegar for at least 1 hour.
2. Grill the lamb chops over medium heat until desired doneness (about 4-5 minutes per side).
3. Serve with steamed rice and stir-fried vegetables.

Soybean Sprout Stir Fry

Ingredients:

- 2 cups soybean sprouts, washed
- 1 tbsp soy sauce
- 1 tsp sesame oil
- 1 tbsp garlic, minced
- 1 tbsp rice vinegar
- 1 tbsp chili paste (optional)
- 1/4 cup green onions, chopped

Instructions:

1. Heat sesame oil in a pan, sauté garlic until fragrant.
2. Add soybean sprouts and stir-fry for 2–3 minutes until tender.
3. Season with soy sauce, rice vinegar, and chili paste. Stir to coat.
4. Garnish with green onions and serve as a side dish.

Beijing Mustard Leaf Stir Fry

Ingredients:

- 2 cups mustard greens, washed and chopped
- 1 tbsp soy sauce
- 1 tbsp oyster sauce
- 1 tbsp sesame oil
- 1 tsp sugar
- 2 cloves garlic, minced

Instructions:

1. Heat sesame oil in a wok, sauté garlic until fragrant.
2. Add mustard greens and stir-fry until wilted, about 5 minutes.
3. Add soy sauce, oyster sauce, and sugar, and stir well.
4. Serve hot as a flavorful side dish.

Water Chestnut Cakes

Ingredients:

- 1 cup water chestnut flour
- 1/2 cup water
- 1 tbsp sugar
- 1 tbsp sesame oil
- 1/4 cup chopped scallions

Instructions:

1. Mix water chestnut flour, water, sugar, and sesame oil to form a smooth batter.
2. Pour the batter into a greased cake pan and steam for 20 minutes.
3. Garnish with chopped scallions before serving.
4. Serve warm as a light snack or dessert.

Cold Garlic Eggplant

Ingredients:

- 2 medium eggplants, sliced into rounds
- 2 tbsp soy sauce
- 1 tbsp rice vinegar
- 1 tbsp sesame oil
- 2 cloves garlic, minced
- 1 tbsp chili oil (optional)
- 1 tbsp chopped cilantro

Instructions:

1. Steam eggplant slices for 10 minutes until soft.
2. Mix soy sauce, rice vinegar, sesame oil, garlic, and chili oil to make the dressing.
3. Toss the steamed eggplant with the dressing.
4. Garnish with chopped cilantro and serve chilled.

Steamed Pork with Rice Powder

Ingredients:

- 1 lb ground pork
- 1/2 cup rice powder
- 1 tbsp soy sauce
- 1 tbsp sesame oil
- 2 cloves garlic, minced
- 1 tbsp ginger, grated
- 2 tbsp chopped green onions

Instructions:

1. Mix ground pork with rice powder, soy sauce, sesame oil, garlic, and ginger.
2. Shape the mixture into small patties or balls.
3. Steam the pork patties for 15–20 minutes until cooked through.
4. Garnish with green onions and serve with steamed rice.

Jujube Red Bean Pudding

Ingredients:

- 1/2 cup red beans, cooked
- 10 jujubes, pitted and chopped
- 1 tbsp sugar
- 1/4 cup water
- 1 tbsp cornstarch (optional for thickening)

Instructions:

1. Cook red beans and jujubes in water until soft.
2. Add sugar and blend the mixture into a smooth paste.
3. If desired, thicken with cornstarch dissolved in a little water.
4. Serve the pudding warm or chilled, garnished with additional chopped jujubes.

Sweet Glutinous Rice Balls

Ingredients:

- 1 cup glutinous rice flour
- 1/4 cup water
- 1 tbsp sugar
- 1/4 cup sweet red bean paste
- 1/4 cup sesame seeds (optional)

Instructions:

1. Mix glutinous rice flour with water and sugar to form a dough.
2. Divide the dough into small portions and fill each with a teaspoon of red bean paste.
3. Roll the balls into smooth shapes.
4. Boil the rice balls in water for 5–7 minutes until they float.
5. Roll them in sesame seeds and serve warm or chilled.

Pickled Radish Salad

Ingredients:

- 2 cups daikon radish, julienned
- 1 tbsp rice vinegar
- 1 tsp sugar
- 1 tbsp soy sauce
- 1/4 tsp chili flakes
- 1 tbsp sesame oil

Instructions:

1. Combine radish, rice vinegar, sugar, soy sauce, and chili flakes in a bowl.
2. Let it sit for at least 30 minutes for the flavors to meld.
3. Drizzle with sesame oil before serving.
4. Serve chilled as a refreshing side dish.

Sesame Flatbread Sandwich

Ingredients:

- 2 cups flour
- 1 tbsp sesame oil
- 1/4 cup warm water
- 1 tbsp sugar
- 1 tsp salt
- 1/4 cup sesame seeds

Instructions:

1. Mix flour, sugar, salt, and warm water to form a dough.
2. Roll dough into flat rounds and cook in a hot, dry pan until golden on both sides.
3. Brush with sesame oil and sprinkle with sesame seeds.
4. Once cooled slightly, use the flatbreads as a sandwich base, filling with your choice of ingredients, such as grilled meat, vegetables, or tofu.

www.ingramcontent.com/pod-product-compliance
Lightning Source LLC
LaVergne TN
LVHW081325060526
838201LV00055B/2469